# RESILIENCE

## FROM CIVIL WAR TO THE CANADIAN DREAM

BY KOMBA KEMBAY

CANADA

Author: Komba Kembay

Printed and bound in Canada

First printing: November 2024

Published by KOMBA KEMBAY

Yukon, Canada

ISBN: 978-1-0691065-6-8 (Paperback)

www.resiliencestorybook.com

# DEDICATION

This book is dedicated to the memory of my late father, Chief Sahr Lebbie Kembay, whose strength and guidance continue to inspire me from beyond. I also honor my elder brother, the late Corporal Tamba Kembay (TK), whose memory remains a guiding light in my journey. I give credit to my mother, my superhero, Sia Sambo Kembay, and my late stepmother, Mama Adama Kembay, whose love and sacrifices have shaped the person I am today. I am deeply grateful to my cousin, Raymond Sahr Finoh, whose unwavering support sustained me during my time in the United States. To my immediate and extended family, your love and encouragement have been the bedrock of my resilience. Finally, I give thanks to God, who has given me the strength and wisdom to complete this book.

# Acknowledgments

One of my greatest blessings is the gift of resilience, which has strengthened me for my family, my wife, and our four amazing children. I hope to pass down this resilience to Abrielle, Paulson, Claudia, and Saphina, as a part of the legacy I leave for you. Daddy loves all of you deeply.

I also wish to express my heartfelt gratitude to those who have stood by me with unwavering support and encouragement:

- Rev. and Mrs. PAC Williams
- Mrs. Sia Yankosa Kembay
- Mr. Alimamy Kargbo

- Ms. Adria Vizzi Holub

- Ms. Isatu Kamara

- Mr. Kai Ngebga

- Mr. Isaac Sahr Sam

- Mr. Samuel A. Koineh

- Mr. and Mrs. Nyakeh Momoh

- Mr. and Mrs. Emmanuel Bope

- Ms. Millicent Deen-Turay

- Ms. Juliet Ify

- Ms. Kumba Rhema Thomas

Thank you all for your steadfast presence in my life.

# Contents

# PREFACE

In *Resilience: From Civil War to The Canadian Dream*, I invite you to embark on a journey that transcends the tumultuous backdrop of my early years in Sierra Leone. My story begins in a country rich with culture, heritage, and a vibrant spirit, yet overshadowed by a decade-long civil war. Forced to seek refuge in displaced-persons and refugee camps, I persevered in pursuing further educational and professional goals, ultimately moving to the United States and then Canada.

While this narrative acknowledges the struggles and pain of conflict, it is essential to emphasize that Sierra Leone is not defined by war. It is a nation of resilience and hope, steadily recovering and flourishing as it embraces its rich history and immense potential.

By sharing my experiences, I hope to inspire those who face their own battles, whether in Sierra Leone, across the African continent, or anywhere in the world. Life's challenges can be daunting, but I believe that resilience is a universal thread that connects us all. Through my story, I wish to offer a message of hope and encourage readers to persevere and find strength in the face of adversity.

May this book serve not only as a testament to my personal journey but also as a beacon for anyone seeking inspiration to navigate their own challenges. Together, let us embrace resilience and the boundless possibilities that await us.

# INTRODUCTION

My life has been marked by trials that could snuff out the spirit, yet they failed to extinguish the flame of hope within me. As a teenager, I navigated the harrowing landscape of a brutal civil war, where every day was a battle for survival. Amidst the chaos, I clung fiercely to my dreams and refused to let the darkness consume me.

I witnessed horrors that would haunt me for a lifetime. People fell around me, their lives stolen by senseless brutality. The sight of severed hands and the sound of gunfire tearing through the air were the nightmares that plagued my reality. Yet, through it all, I refused to surrender to despair. I held fast to the belief that there was still a future, still a path forward. I pressed forward and ran for my life, determined to escape and bear witness to the atrocities I had seen.

The loss of my father, my pillar of strength, could have shattered me. But still, I carried on and honored his memory with tenacity and determination.

Displacement became my new reality as I sought refuge in camps and foreign lands. Despite the uncertainty and adversity, I remained steadfast in my resolve.

I endured a bitter cold winter without any heat in a new country. The trials of everyday life in this new country tested my endurance, but they could not break me. I emerged from each challenge stronger and more resilient than before.

And when the world seemed to turn its back on me, when doubt and uncertainty threatened to consume me, I refused to be defined by others' perceptions. I clung to my dreams with unwavering determination.

This book is a testament to the power of resilience, a beacon of hope for those who find themselves in the darkest of nights. No matter the obstacles you face, no matter the odds stacked against you, know this: resilience is your greatest ally. Hold fast to your dreams, for they are the light that will guide you through the storm. Do not give up. You are capable of more than you realize.

## My Definition of Resilience

Resilience is choosing to work towards a better tomorrow, even in the midst of great hardships today.

# CHAPTER 1:
# NGANDORHUN

I am from the small, quiet town of Ngandorhun, which is nestled in the Gbane Chiefdom, Kono district, in the far eastern reaches of Sierra Leone. The area is characterized by a mix of forested regions and agricultural lands, with a tropical climate that includes a rainy season and a dry season.

The town is predominantly inhabited by members of the Kono ethnic group, one of the small ethnic groups in Sierra Leone. The Kono people have a rich cultural heritage, including their own language, traditional music, dance, and storytelling. The primary language spoken in Ngandorhun is Kono, although Krio and English (the official language of Sierra Leone) are also commonly understood. The economy of Ngandorhun is largely based on agriculture. Residents engage in subsistence farming, growing crops such as rice, cassava, cocoa, coffee, and various fruits and vegetables. The region is also known for its palm oil production. In addition to agriculture, some inhabitants are involved in small-scale trading, fishing, and artisanal mining, particularly for gold.

Ngandorhun faces several development challenges, including poverty, limited access to healthcare and education, and infrastructure deficits. Even so, the town also has potential for growth, particularly through sustainable agricultural practices, small-scale mining, and community-driven development projects.

The people of Ngandorhun are known for their hospitality and strong sense of community. Social bonds are reinforced through communal activities, cooperative farming, and shared participation in cultural events. Community leadership often involves elders and traditional leaders, who play a vital role in decision-making and conflict resolution.

Ngandorhun is a town that embodies the rich cultural heritage and resilient spirit of Sierra Leone. While it faces significant challenges, efforts to improve infrastructure, education, and economic opportunities continue its development.

Childhood in Ngandorhun was replete with joyous moments and cherished memories. We organized group swimming programs, fishing trips, and small sports activities, such as neighborhood soccer competitions. Under the moonlit sky, we reveled in laughter, shared jokes, and engaged in spirited games. Some evenings, the air was filled with the rhythm of traditional music, which beckoned us to dance and celebrate. The dry season, with its bright moon and star-studded canopy, held a special allure and cast a magical glow over our nighttime escapades.

My parents, Chief Sahr Lebbie Kembay and Sia Sambo Kembay, laid the foundation of my life in this serene setting. My father started his career as a commercial driver, then later ventured into mining. He amassed the bulk of our family's fortune through his ventures in diamonds and gold, primarily in the bustling town of Saidu, Sandor Chiefdom. With his newfound wealth, he invested in properties across major cities in Sierra Leone and indulged in luxury cars, which marked his ascent in societal standing.

Eventually, my father felt the pull of his familial roots and returned to Ngandorhun, Gbane Chiefdom, where he met my mother, and they embarked on a journey of marriage.

My father desired to serve his people. Philanthropy coursed through his veins, a trait that endeared him to many. He competed for the position of chiefdom speaker and emerged victorious, which earned him the people's adoration and esteem. The Gbane Chiefdom political hierarchy is led by the paramount chief. The next in authority is the chiefdom speaker (my dad), who is over the section chiefs, the town chiefs, and the chiefdom elders. My father ascended to the esteemed position of chiefdom speaker—a mantle he bore with honor until the curtain of life fell upon him.

In the annals of Ngandorhun, my father, the late Chief Sahr Lebbie Kembay, was a beacon of hope, not only to my young heart but to the entire kinship. He possessed a charm and magnetism that drew people to him like moths to flame. Among his treasures were five wives, each as resplendent and beloved as the next, my own mother among them.

By the time I arrived into this world, my father had already ascended the throne of chieftaincy. His abode in Ngandorhun burgeoned with life. Its halls echoed with the laughter of kinfolk and friends, and each house within his compound teemed with occupants. Such was his sway over the chiefdom that the elders sought his counsel every dawn, and their deliberations were a testament to his wisdom and sagacity.

## The Kembay Compound

The Kembay compound in Ngandorhun was renowned for several reasons: it was the chief's compound, comprised of three houses, home to over twenty people. Each house had a distinct role, which reflected the structure of our family. My father's five wives each had their own rooms. My father resided in the central house, which was known as the main building. The wives were ranked according to the order in which they married my father. The first wife, Mama Adama, was the most senior. My mother, Sia Sambo Kembay (née Amara), was his third wife.

To this day, I marvel at how my father managed to maintain harmony and respect within such a large family. Mama Adama commanded respect from the other wives, and my father was equally revered. Remarkably, I never witnessed any of the wives fighting or even disagreeing. It was a peaceful environment.

The main house had five bedrooms. It was occupied by my father, his first wife, my father's elder brother, Pa Moimo, and his elder sister, Kumba Kembay (commonly known as "Nurse MK"). There was also a common room for teenage boys. The other two houses were occupied by the other four wives and close family members.

In those days, there was no concept of storing food in a refrigerator. Every day, my father would give money to ensure that food was prepared for more than twenty people living in the compound. A fifty-kilogram (110-

pound) bag of rice would last only three or four days, and we consumed almost eight bags of rice every month. It was astonishing, especially considering that none of my father's wives worked outside of the home, except for the youngest and most junior wife, who was a nurse. The rest were full-time housewives.

The wives took turns cooking on a three-day cycle. My father gave the money to the first wife, who then handed it to the wife responsible for cooking that day. Occasionally, the first wife chose to cook herself. The food was called "foloba," but I have no idea how this name originated, and no one has explained it to me to this day.

I still remember the sight of over twenty dishes served in different bowls. It was quite a scene when the dishes were distributed. The teenage boys ate together from a large bowl, as did the teenage girls. Every day, many elders visited my father. My father's food was on a large tray or bowl, and he would eat with the elders from the same dish.

The Kembay compound was a training ground for me. My half-siblings, the neighborhood boys, and I engaged in activities such as swimming, hiking, and backyard soccer games. Some days, we would invite other boys from the area to the nearby playground, where we would engage in one-on-one fights until a champion emerged. For example, I would fight my brother, and if I defeated him, he would be out of the contest, and I would move on to the next opponent. The last one standing would be crowned the champion for the week.

When I was young, one of my closest uncles, Tamba Amara, commonly known as "Pastor," often invited me to go fishing with him. He was very experienced, and I was just learning. Whenever we went fishing, he caught lots of fish, while I usually went home empty-handed. Sometimes, he made fun of me and laughed at my lack of success. One day, when we went fishing, he caught many fish and secured them on a special rope we had prepared. Then he told me we should go back in the water and continue fishing. A little while later, the current became stronger and swept all of the fish he had caught off the rope. He was very upset, but I felt a little happy because now neither of us had any fish. I wanted to laugh, but I was afraid he would get angry. We continued fishing, and after a while, he caught more fish, and I caught a few too. We both went home happy that day.

## Road Trips with Dad

My brother Wurie and I reveled in our father's company and trailed after him like eager acolytes on a pilgrimage. Together, we traversed the neighboring towns and basked in the camaraderie of his kinsmen. Those were halcyon days, suffused with the warmth of paternal love and the promise of a boundless future. The most common places we visited were the small towns of Fadima and Taiya, where my father had a strong extended family and supporter base. We were always happy to accompany him to these places because his kinsmen would give us gifts such as goats, sheep, chickens, and sometimes smoked meat from wild animals they'd hunted. We especially enjoyed homemade food prepared with the game meat. My brother and I always got excited when our dad told us we were traveling to those small towns. We were treated with the utmost respect and made friends each time we visited.

## Lessons From My Father

Amidst the ebb and flow of daily life, my father imparted the following invaluable lessons:

He taught me to treat people with respect and dignity and to treat elders with even more respect. He stressed the importance of showing love and commitment to my siblings, my mom, and other family members.

He said, "Komba, respect everyone and treat them well, but never allow anyone to bully you because it will dampen your spirit and sometimes make you weak. Always stand for what you know is right."

He taught me to value my family. He told me that family should always work together as a team.

He taught me not to run away from problems. He explained that if I avoided the problems I was supposed to resolve, they would haunt me later in life. He encouraged me to be bold and optimistic about life, even in the face of difficulties.

He taught me when to be serious and hard-working and when to be relaxed and playful.

He taught me generosity, resilience, and un-wavering fortitude. I witnessed his acts of kindness and compassion. For example, every year during the rainy season, which is always difficult, my father bought bags of rice to freely give to people who needed assistance. I watched my father's actions and gleaned insights into the true essence of leadership, which taught me how to navigate the complexities of human nature with grace and humility.

Even in the shadow of conflict, my father remained steadfast in his commitment to his family and his community. His unwavering resolve was a beacon of hope amidst the encroaching darkness. Once, he was betrayed by the people he confided in and trusted the most. Some of his friends conspired to make false allegations that got him detained at the police station for a few hours. As a young boy, I saw this betrayal firsthand. I spoke with my dad when he was released from the police station, wanting to know why he was there and why I wasn't allowed to see him. He told me, "Komba, my colleagues, chiefs, and others conspired to cause me problems." He didn't explain what happened in detail; I suppose he thought I was too young to be told more. As I grew older, I realized that my dad was protecting my mental health by not giving me more information than I could handle.

As the winds of war swept across our land, my father's steadfast courage was my guiding light, illuminating the path forward amidst the chaos. Little did I know our time together was drawing to a close.

# Chapter 2:
# Primary Education

I attended United Methodist Church Primary School for first through seventh grade. Primary school days were filled with anticipation. Each morning, I eagerly rose from the bed and knew my mother would prepare a good breakfast, such as fried plantain and fish with gravy made from sliced onions and fresh tomatoes or yams with game meat stew. Our school was a few kilometers away from our home. Sometimes, our elders kindly gave my brothers and me a ride, but I cherished the days when I could walk to school. There were two main routes: the bustling main motor road and a quieter shortcut through the coffee and cocoa gardens. The shortcut offered tranquility, a refreshing breeze, and chirping birds.

School typically ended at 2:00 p.m., which coincided with the sun's scorching heat. Walking home along the main road meant enduring a long journey under the blazing sun, which left one exhausted and drenched in sweat when one finally reached home. Most of us preferred the shady path through the coffee and cocoa trees.

I remember one intriguing character from lunchtime at school: a large, imposing student who never brought his own lunch. As soon as the lunch bell rang, he swiftly made his way to the communal eating area, where most of us gathered to enjoy our meals. This individual moved from person to person and helped himself with portions of their lunch. He warned anyone who refused to share, "Make sure you don't take the shortcut home today; I'll be waiting for those who don't share." Menaced by his ultimatum, many reluctantly parted with a portion of their lunch to avoid the long journey home under the unforgiving sun.

I was appointed as the class prefect during primary school, in both third and fifth grade, despite my small stature among my larger peers. As a prefect, it was my responsibility to maintain order in the classroom when the teacher was absent. Because of my small stature, I befriended one of the larger boys, Tamba Jimissa, to protect and fight for me. With his presence beside me, I kept the class under control when the teacher was away.

Primary school in Sierra Leone was fiercely competitive, particularly in the upper grades (fifth through seventh), which were the final years before graduating to secondary school. One notable aspect of this contest was the "hot mental" sessions, during which the class teacher challenged us to recite multiplication tables or answer rapid-fire arithmetic questions. These daily exercises compelled me to study diligently before each class.

After primary school, I eagerly sat for the national selective entrance exams, which determined secondary school enrollment. Sadly, my excitement was quickly overshadowed by the outbreak of the brutal civil war, which disrupted the educational journey of all students across the nation.

# CHAPTER 3:
# THE SIERRA LEONE CIVIL WAR

In the pre-dawn hours of 1991, the tranquility of our home in Ngandorhun was shattered by a cacophony of gunfire. Startled from our slumber, fear coiled around us, leaving us breathless and terrified. With each burst of gunfire, danger loomed ever closer until it became an undeniable reality. Rebels had descended upon our town and left chaos and destruction in their wake.

We were forced to flee with nothing but the clothes on our backs. We sought refuge in the unforgiving embrace of the wilderness, our footsteps muffled by the weight of uncertainty and grief. Tears mingled with dust as we wandered aimlessly, haunted by the specter of an uncertain future. The news of our ancestral home being consumed by flames struck a grievous blow to my father's spirit. Anguish was etched upon his face—a poignant testament to the irreplaceable losses we had suffered.

Days turned into weeks as we traversed treacherous terrain. We sought sanctuary wherever it could be found. We arrived in the town of Koidu, the harsh crucible of our displacement. The most basic necessities had become elusive luxuries. Yet, amid the turmoil, the desire for education burned bright within my brother Wurie and me and drove us to seek opportunities for learning amidst the chaos.

Our elder sister, Kumba, introduced us to entrepreneurship. The goal was to supplement our funds so we could pay our secondary education fees and buy school materials and shoes. For weeks, our sister arose at 6 a.m. to fry puff cakes with a delicious sauce made of grounded dry fish, onion, and spicy pepper. The cakes were divided between Wurie and me, and we went to the nearby communities and sold them individually to raise the needed money. We recruited and retained loyal customers through this business, and some bought from us daily. Members from one of our local and most popular soccer teams, the Diamond Stars, became our most loyal customers. We learned valuable life skills, such as communication, marketing, and how to build business relationships. We were committed and fondly engaged in this business until schools were about to start. Thanks to our sister and our community, we raised the needed cash to fund our early secondary school education. As we progressed through the ranks of secondary school, each milestone achieved was a beacon of hope.

## My Mom, My Superhero

Amidst the escalating civil war and adversity, my mother shouldered the immense responsibility of providing for six children. As a teenager attending secondary school, I recall my mother borrowing a five-gallon container of palm oil from the local suppliers at the Tankoro market. She tirelessly sold this oil in a stall at the market, under the scorching sun, until late afternoon, then used the meager profits to purchase food to cook for our family.

I often accompanied my mother to the local

marketplace to assist her in selling. On one oc-
casion, after school, I visited my mother at the
marketplace and saw the tiredness on her face.
I noticed my mother's feet were mildly swol-
len from prolonged sitting. I felt so bad for my
mother, but there was nothing I could do. I re-
treated to a secluded spot and wept silently. I
was unwilling to burden my mother with my
sorrow.

# Chapter 4: The Displaced-Persons Camp

In April 1992, between 7 and 10 a.m., heavy gunfire pierced the air. The rebels had reached Koidu. We thought we were safe, that perhaps the worst was behind us. We didn't know our ordeal had only begun. The streets were littered with lifeless bodies, and crimson pools stained the ground—a testament to the brutality of war. With fear gnawing at our hearts, we navigated through the chaos and clung to survival with every step. We gathered only our essentials and fled the city, embarking on a harrowing journey that would span hundreds of miles.

In our frantic flight, my mother accounted for the safety of each family member before fleeing. As a teenager with younger siblings, I was ill-prepared for the challenges that lay ahead. I had no choice but to grow up and help my mom to take care of my younger siblings. It was a difficult task because I was only a teenager and still figuring things out myself. I had to learn leadership and patience. Some days, I got frustrated and even fought with my siblings. One day, I was so upset with my brother Kai that I threw a big stone at him. Fortunately, he was not hit. If that stone had hit him, there he could have been disfigured, or worse. To this day, I am grateful to God that the stone did not hit him.

For days, we sought refuge wherever we could and bedded down on bare mats along road-sides in small villages and towns. Community centers and places of worship were places we would look for shelter first whenever we arrived at a new location. We stayed in those villages and towns for hours, sometimes days, but we never lingered long. There was no safe place for us to settle down.

Eventually, we arrived in Masingbi, where we found sanctuary in a displaced persons camp. With assistance from the Sierra Leone Red Cross Society, we erected makeshift tents, which were little more than trampolines draped with tarps. They provided scant shelter for my mother, siblings, uncles, aunts, and countless other displaced families. Privacy was a luxury we could no longer afford, and survival became our sole focus.

Life in the camp was a daily struggle for existence. The daily weight of uncertainty of each
new day was compounded by the constant
scarcity of food. We relied on the support of
organizations such as the Sierra Leone Red
Cross Society, and registered as displaced persons in order to access meager rations. We
stood in lines for hours under the burning sun
to get the supplies: corn mills, corn flour,
beans, dried packeted fish, bulgur, and cooking oil. After receiving our allotment, we returned to our respective tents, prepared the
food, and ate with our family. Even then, sustenance was always insufficient. My mother
sold her most prized possessions, jewelry, and
clothing, to augment our provisions. She
watched over us as we ate and contented herself with what little remained. She endured
days of hunger to ensure that her children

were fed. This daily sacrifice defined her unwavering commitment to our wellbeing throughout our displacement.

Through these trials, my bond with my mother deepened, and my admiration for her grew immeasurably. I resolved that upon completing my education and securing employment, I would honor her sacrifices by providing her with a comfortable retirement.

I am profoundly grateful to God for blessing me with such an extraordinary mother. She is not only my best friend, but also my superhero. Mama, your love and sacrifices will forever be remembered and cherished. I love you dearly.

Amidst the despair and deprivation, my faith in a brighter tomorrow wavered. Lost in the shadows of the displaced persons camp, thoughts of death sometimes consumed my mind. It felt like an eternity spent in purgatory.

Life became meaningless; there was nothing productive to do. I started hanging out with a bad crowd of much older men. They had a particular place on the outskirts of the camp where they assembled every day to smoke marijuana, drink palm wine, and talk about politics. I started frequenting their gatherings, and their perspective began to influence me.

One day, I sat with them while they were smoking marijuana, and I got so high I felt as if I had been smoking it myself. After a few months of attending their gatherings, one of the guys gave me marijuana to smoke, and I did. That night, I was very high, and I slept like a baby, but when I woke up, I was super hungry and had no food to eat. It was crazy. I told myself I wouldn't smoke weed again, but I continued smoking for a few more weeks until, one day, I made a conscious decision to stop.

Later, I was introduced to palm wine, and I drank it throughout my stay at the displaced-persons camp. I would usually get money to buy palm wine from selling some of our food supplies, such as cooking oil and beans, to the locals of Masingbi.

This camp life taught me a valuable lesson as I grew into adulthood: you can get involved in bad habits due to situations beyond your control or from being influenced by people you consider friends.

## Return to Koidu

Sometime between 1994 and 1995, Koidu was declared safe again. With cautious optimism, we returned to the city and hoped to reclaim a semblance of normalcy that had been torn from us. Wurie and I started attending Koidu Secondary School. I was in tenth grade, and my brother was in ninth grade.

# Chapter 5:

# The Death of My Father

In 1995, I started tenth grade at Koidu Secondary School. Life, though marred by civil war, had begun to find its rhythm once more, and there were glimpses of normalcy amidst the chaos. Evenings spent in the company of my father, his laughter a balm to my weary soul, were cherished memories, a testament to the enduring bond between father and son.

My father had resumed diamond mining operations along the bank of the Sawafe River. Beneath the veneer of normalcy, a palpable tension simmered. Despite his stoic I, I sensed the weight of the world that pressed down upon my father's shoulders. His inner turmoil foreshadowed the challenges that lay ahead.

In April 1995, amidst the spirited fervor of our school's annual multi-sport event, I was tasked with representing my beloved Blue sport house in the rigorous 100-meter sprint. Wurie and I, comrades in both blood and ambition, ran together in this pursuit. Alas, such endeavors required resources, and it was our father, who was laboring at the diamond mining site in Babakunaya, who held the purse strings.

On the morning of April 8th, a Saturday like any other, I traveled from the town of Koidu to the mining site to seek his counsel and support. When I arrived at his side, he embraced me with a gleam of paternal pride in his eyes. We wended our way through the mining grounds, while he explained the nuances of his labor and showed me the fruits of his endeavors. In a moment of shared intimacy, he apprised me of a significant discovery — a treasure trove of diamonds that promised to reshape our family's fortunes.

As the day waned and the sun dipped low on the horizon, a premonition stirred within me, which urged a swift return to our home in Koidu. My father, resolute in his plans, insisted on remaining until the next day. Little did I know that those moments would be our final exchange, our last embrace, our ultimate farewell.

On the dawn of April 9th, in the midst of my morning preparations, Gbanma, my elder brother Sahr's wife, who was staying at the mining site, came to Koidu and told me that my father had died. He was found in his bed by our elder brother Sahr, and it was assumed he had died of natural causes. As our country was in the throes of civil war, there was no way to have a postmortem done. The news of my father's passing struck me like a thunderbolt and left me numb and bereft. Shirtless and disoriented, I stumbled into a cacophony of grief, my anguished cries stifled by the embrace of well-meaning kin.

Hours later, as my father's lifeless body lay in repose within the confines of our home, the weight of his absence settled upon me like a leaden shroud. Here was the titan, his unassailable strength rendered inert by the cruel hand of fate. In the desolate expanse of that moment, I sought solace in memories—the whispered conversations, the shared laughter, the bond of filial love that had tethered us together.

Grief was relentless in its onslaught. The specter of civil war loomed large and cast its shadow over our mourning. The imperative to lay my father to rest in his cherished chiefdom town of Ngandorhun was fraught with peril. Trepidation was our constant companion as we made our trek, guided by the steely resolve of my father's high-ranking military younger brother, Colonel Sahr Sinah, whose authority commanded respect even amidst the chaos of war.

In the hushed stillness of Ngandorhun, amidst the whispers of the fallen and the echoes of a once vibrant community, we consigned my father's body to his final resting place — a poignant testament to his legacy of leadership and love. As we retraced our steps, the hollow emptiness of our loss lingered, a silent sentinel of the aching void left in the wake of his passing.

As I commit these words to paper twenty-eight years later, the ache of his absence persists unabated. Even in death, my dear father, Chief Sahr Lebbie Kembay, endures—his indomitable spirit is present forever in my memory. Rest in peace, beloved patriarch. Your legacy lives on in the hearts of those who loved you most.

Unfortunately, his life ended during the Sierra Leone Civil War, and his properties were ravaged by rebel forces. In those times, it was rare for people to consider investing or saving money in banks. With his passing, our financial stability vanished. We were left destitute and without aid. Even my father's closest friends turned their backs on us.

# CHAPTER 6:
# THE REFUGEE CAMP

In 1995, a few months after my dad passed away, my elder brother Tamba Kembay (affectionately known as TK) brought Wurie and me to stay with our other elder brother Tamba Lebbie Kembay (affectionately known as "Tamba Police") in Freetown, the capital city of Sierra Leone. TK is my brother from the same father. Tamba Police is my father's younger brother's son. Technically, Tamba Police is my cousin, but in my culture, I would refer to him as my brother, which is completely acceptable.

Corporal Tamba Kembay joined the army at a young age to serve his country and demonstrated bravery, familial dedication, and a strong work ethic. He selflessly sacrificed his military salary to finance me and Wurie's relocation to the country's capital, Freetown, for schooling. Tamba Police was a traffic police officer. Despite financial hardship, TK and Tamba Police ensured we were able to go to high school. Our big brother Sahr Kembay, fondly called Gipo, provided us with additional financial and moral support whilst we were in Freetown. Thank you, big brothers.

Our elder sister, Yainkain Sesay, facilitated our enrollment into a school dedicated to underprivileged children, which was located at the extreme end of Freetown. The school provided us with a meal daily, which alleviated one of our financial burdens. The distance to school posed a significant challenge, and we often had to walk due to the cost of transportation. My brother and I stayed in that school until I completed eleventh grade, and he completed tenth grade. After one year, TK's financial standing improved, which enabled us to transition to a school closer to home. I am forever grateful to TK, Tamba Police, Gipo, and Yainkain.

During those school days, there were two important daily struggles: transportation and food. I walked to school over 90% of the time. Sometimes, we visited nearby family members, hoping to get additional food. One such person was T. E. Finoh. He was a very funny old man, and he would call my brother Will Will instead of Wurie.

One day, at our new school, Ahmadiyya Secondary School, in Kissy Dockyard, I bumped into one of our childhood friends/cousins, Sahr Thomas. We were from the same town, Ngandorhun, and had attended the same primary school. He told me he was having difficulties with his accommodation. My brother and I decided to take him into our small living space.

Whilst preparing for the General Certificate Examination Ordinary Level (GCE 'O') exams, the Armed Forces Revolutionary Council (AFRC) overthrew the legitimate Sierra Leone People's Party (SLPP) government led by Ahmad Tejan Kabba. The Junta government initially stationed themselves in the capital city, Freetown. Freetown became very unstable because of the Junta rule. Immediately after I finished taking my GCE 'O', Wurie and I decided to go back to Koidu, while Sahr went to Bo, his mother's hometown.

In the early months of 1998, Koidu once again fell victim to brutal rebel attacks, which prompted us to seek sanctuary in the neighboring country of Guinea. My mother was thrust into the dual role of both mother and father, tasked with guiding us through the horrors of civil war.

We traversed forests and small towns, evaded rebel pursuit, and endured unimaginable hardships for months. The constant threat of violence hung over us like a dark cloud. The memory of families consumed by flames in nearby bushes haunted our every waking moment. We slept in community centers and places of worship, and sometimes, kind-hearted locals would let us sleep in their living rooms or on their balconies. We stayed in those villages and towns for a few days to rest, then continued our journey to Guinea. Sleep was now a luxury, replaced by restless nights on high alert for rebel incursions. We ran for our lives. Children's cries echoed our own desperation, and the elderly succumbed to exhaustion along the arduous trek, their weary bodies unable to endure the miles.

After what felt like an eternity of flight, we reached the Sierra Leone-Guinea border. There, we were screened by Guinean authorities before being permitted to cross into their country. We were transported by UNHCR trucks to the Massakondou Refugee Camp, which became our new temporary home.

The UNHCR provided emergency rations and tarp shelters, where my mother, siblings, and I shared a common space devoid of privacy, again. We navigated the bureaucratic processes of registering with the UNHCR for essential supplies to survive.

After several months under makeshift tents, we attempted to construct more permanent dwellings. We gathered materials from nearby forests and bushes and toiled to erect rudimentary mud and stick huts. These lodgings were a tangible symbol of our determination to rebuild amidst adversity.

Life in the camp was marked by daily struggles. Essential items were a long walk away in the main town of Kissidougu. My mother worked tirelessly to provide for our family. As a teenager, I keenly felt the weight of her burden and resolved to alleviate it.

Through resourcefulness and determination, I became an entrepreneur again and learned the intricacies of trading solid ball soap from a fellow refugee, Ibrahim Jalloh. Ibrahim also spoke the Guinean local language. He introduced me to a few soap suppliers who lived in the main city of Kissidougou, which was approximately nine kilometers (five and a half miles) outside of the refugee camp.

Every morning, I woke up at 5:30 a.m., got myself ready, walked to Kissidougou to buy a few dozen balls of soap, and then walked back to the refugee camp, stopping at the neighboring villages and towns to sell the soap. I went from house to house and honed my salesmanship and communication skills in the local language. I had to be in villages by 7 a.m.; otherwise, the locals would have gone to their respective farms. I traveled to places I had little or no clue about. I could have been kidnapped or eaten by a wild animal. There were days I felt terrified while walking alone in the middle of the forest. Even so, I trusted in God on a daily basis and the spirit of resilience kept me going. Days turned into months as I navigated the challenges of my new trade, and I used the proceeds to help my mom support our family's needs.

Amidst the daily grind, a glimmer of hope emerged. The UNHCR announced plans to repatriate young students back to Sierra Leone for continued education. Recognizing the opportunity for a brighter future, Wurie and I seized the chance, supported by our mother's blessing.

More months passed while we awaited repatriation, during which I redoubled my efforts to provide for my family. Finally, in June 1998, we were repatriated to Freetown and left behind the now-familiar confines of the refugee camp. Though the decision weighed heavily on my heart, I knew it was a necessary step towards a better tomorrow.

Leaving the camp meant severing communication with my mother and siblings, which was a painful sacrifice during a time without modern technology. Even so, in the face of uncertainty, we clung to hope and trusted that our paths would one day converge again.

In the first week of July 1998, Wurie and I safely arrived back in Freetown. We decided to check the place where we had lived before. Coincidentally, we met our childhood friend/cousin Sahr Thomas again, with whom we had lost communication for over a year. The landlord told us that the apartment was no longer available for us to rent. We had no other place to go, so we were practically homeless. For a week, we slept at different places in Freetown with friends. We turned to my mother's younger sister, Aunt Doris, as a last resort.

## Life at Aunty Doris '

Aunt Jane Doris Lebbie and her husband, BKB Lebbie, compassionately agreed to shelter us. Aunty Doris' place was packed with displaced people, mostly from the Kono district. Food was scarce, and sleeping arrangements were cramped. We kept our clothes in the annex building where some guys were living and slept in the living room of the main building. We were the last ones to go to bed at night and the first ones to get up in the morning. Wurie, Sahr Thomas, and I were all Muslims. However, since we were living with our aunt, whose husband was a pastor, we participated in nightly prayer time and morning devotional sessions. This is when we gave our lives to Jesus and became Christians.

One popular feature in the yard was the big hand pump for the water well. This well was a major source of clean drinking water for our household and the entire community. We were responsible for fetching water and ensuring our household had enough for cooking and for use in all of the bathrooms. After fetching water for our family, we would bring water to other households. Our new role made us popular in the community. These people invited us into their houses and gave us food to eat.

Our situation was so dire that people in our own household called us the "suffering masses." We didn't take it personally. Aunt Doris encouraged me to persevere. She recognized my potential and instilled hope in me. Her loving guidance helped me remain focused on my studies.

In November 1998, Sahr Thomas and I were preparing to take the final General Certificate

Examination to complete our college requirements. One night, while studying, we were so hungry that we couldn't focus. Grandma Maitta came into the living room, and we told her we were too hungry to study. She brought us homemade garri, a porridge-like dish made from ground cassava roots, but we needed sugar to mix with it. Sahr poured some water into the garri, and we waited for our grandma to bring the sugar. Our good and kind-hearted grandma mistakenly brought us raw soda instead. She had just woken up from sleep in the middle of the night to check on us, and the raw soda looked like sugar because both were white. For some reason, I decided to dip my finger into it and put it on my tongue. It burned, so I told Sahr to do the same. He did, and it burned his tongue too. We then realized it was raw soda, not sugar! Our hunger disappeared immediately. We realized that if we had mixed that soda into the garri and eaten it, it could have been the end of our lives. We reassured grandma that it was not her fault. We told her not to feel bad, as she was just trying to help her grandsons. I eventually passed my second attempt at the GCE 'O' Level exams, which paved the way for university studies.

## Zainab Kama Braima (Aunty Kay)

After meeting the academic requirements for university, financial concerns threatened to derail my aspirations. Determined to pursue higher education, I applied to both my preferred school, the Institute of Public Administration and Management (IPAM), with a focus on accounting, and to the more affordable Milton Margai Teachers College. I was accepted into both. Because my funds were limited, I reluctantly opted for the latter, supported only by partial assistance for the first semester's fees. An intervention from one of my childhood friends, Sahr Augustine Musa, who was a second-year student at the time, provided temporary relief. He secured us shared accommodation and meals. During this time, I formed valuable friendships with my classmates while we studied and worked on school assignments together. One notable friend was Davies Nbayo, who provided guidance and support during this challenging period.

Three weeks into my studies, my newfound friend/brother, Davies Nbayo, introduced me to Mrs. Zainab Kama Braima, affectionately known as Aunty Kay or Aunty Zain. Aunty Kay noticed I struggled to obtain food and school supplies, so she graciously invited me to stay with her family. She offered much-needed stability and support. I immersed myself in her household and found solace amidst the warmth of her family, including her husband, Mr. Keikurah Briama. Aunty Kay's unwavering support extended beyond accommodation. Upon learning about my accounting aspirations, she generously offered to fund my education at my preferred college, IPAM. Overwhelmed with gratitude, I embarked on my accounting studies at IPAM, buoyed by her selfless act of kindness. Aunty Kay's continued guidance and encouragement launched my academic and personal growth to the next level and shaped the trajectory of my future.

# CHAPTER 7:
# FROM SIERRA LEONE TO NORTH AMERICA

The Sierra Leone civil war was officially declared over in 2001.

Upon graduating from university, I started my professional career in Sierra Leone as an audit associate with KPMG International, one of the four largest accounting organizations. I dedicated myself to KPMG for three years before transitioning to a non-governmental organization (NGO), where I worked as the finance administrator and finance manager. I returned to the heart of my homeland, Kono, which was deeply scarred by the civil war. At the NGO, through prudent financial management and proper resource allocations, I contributed to providing psychosocial services for survivors of war atrocities, which was a profound opportunity to serve my people. I traveled extensively across the 14 chiefdoms of Kono and engaged with chiefs and local leaders.

I returned to Freetown after a year, where the NGO's headquarters were situated. My tenure there was rewarding and was supported by generous compensation and benefits. With the good pay I received as the finance manager, I saved enough money to construct a 3-bedroom bungalow for my mother in 2010 and fulfilled my pledge to give her some well-deserved respite after years of toiling to raise my siblings and me. I also funded the higher education of a few of my siblings. However, after several years of working with the NGO, I felt the pull to explore the world beyond Sierra Leone and ultimately decided to venture to the United States in 2012.

## Life in the United States

During my initial foray into the United States, I visited various cities. I spent time reconnecting with friends and loved ones. Interestingly, the challenges of life in America were rarely discussed during these visits.

First, I resided with a cousin in Los Angeles, California, who graciously extended her hospitality. Then, I relocated to Kansas City, Missouri, to stay with a younger cousin. Here, the true essence of American life unfolded, which was characterized by financial struggle and daily hardships. Despite my cousin's diligence, making ends meet was elusive. The specter of rent and bills loomed large.

One month, my cousin was unable to pay his rent, so the apartment manager came and banged on our door. We quietly went into the bathroom and stood there until the man left. The rental office was located at the entrance of the driveway for the apartment building, so my cousin had to speed past the office in his car, as if he was in a movie.

## A Week Without Heat

The idyllic image I had of American life was completely shattered when I had to endure a week in a dark, unheated apartment during winter. Nights were eerily silent when I descended to the basement laundry room. I clutched my phone and charger and sought solace in the faint warmth of the electrical socket. It was a harrowing experience. I am uncertain how I managed to endure. During daylight hours, I camped out in nearby shopping centers, braving the bitter cold as I navigated this trying period.

After a few months in the United States, I reconnected with a longtime friend who encouraged me to relocate to Canada. I listened.

# CHAPTER 8:
# THE CANADIAN JOURNEY

Arriving in Canada was both exciting and overwhelming. The vastness of the land, the cold winters, and the fast-paced life were all new to me. I chose to embrace it with the same resilience that had seen me through the war. I worked hard, took on multiple jobs, and never stopped pushing forward. Canada gave me the opportunity to start afresh and to build a new life for myself and my family.

My first job in Canada was in construction. I met a guy at the local church I was attending, and he told me that the construction company he worked for was hiring general laborers. He asked me to meet him at the construction site. Upon my arrival, I was introduced to one of the hiring team members, who gave me a form to fill out. Soon after, I was called to start the job. It was winter, and I happily began. The job paid well, but after a few weeks, I knew it wasn't something I wanted to do long-term.

I joined a recruitment agency and filled out an application online. After a week, I was called to interview for a warehouse position. I passed the interview and started working there. After a month on the floor as a warehouse associate, I approached my supervisor and asked if I could be trained to operate a forklift and a standing reach. My supervisor approved it and sent me for a day of forklift and reach training. I quickly mastered forklift and reach operations and was assigned to the warehouse sales counter. In six months, I was fully hired by the warehouse company, with full benefits.

Determined to grow in the Canadian workplace, I applied to TD Bank. Three months after the application, I received a call from a representative of TD Bank. I did the first phone interview, and two weeks later, I received another call for a second interview. After a month, I was invited to an in-person interview at the TD corporate office. I successfully passed the third and final interview, as well as the police background and other screening checks. I was offered a full-time credit assistant position in the mortgage department at the Western Credit Centre, a department within TD Bank.

I worked for exactly one year at the warehouse before moving to TD Bank. I started to see the light in my Canadian dream. Next, I wanted to go to university to get a Canadian degree. When I shared this aspiration with some of my friends, they questioned why I would want to go to college again when I already had a good job with TD Bank. My response was that the job at TD Bank was just a stepping stone and that if I put in more effort, I could get an even better job. It is important to know what you want in life and pursue it.

In Africa, my educational journey ended with an associate degree in accounting. Some friends cautioned me that I might be deemed too old for undergraduate studies because I was in my thirties, but I was undeterred. Age, in my opinion, should never hinder the pursuit of education. Determined to both enhance my prospects in the Canadian job market and fulfill my aspiration of attaining a university degree, I embarked on this new endeavor with unwavering resolve.

I consulted with an immigrant education advisor and initiated the process of converting my Sierra Leonean educational credentials to Canadian equivalents. After several months, the International Qualifications Assessment Services (IQAS) validated my academic background for Canadian standards. With this equivalency in hand, I applied to the University of Lethbridge's Bachelor of Management program and was fortunate to secure admission.

I applied for a leave of absence from TD Bank to embark on my university journey. Since I was still a relatively new employee at the bank, they approved my leave of absence with no pay. I sacrificed the pay to fulfill my dream.

Relocating to Lethbridge, I secured shared accommodation in close proximity to the university. When I stepped into my first class, I found myself in a sea of youthful faces—a stark contrast to my own. I didn't allow this age gap to dishearten me. I recognized the transient nature of my academic pursuit and remained focused on my goals, determined to acclimatize to the Canadian educational system while immersing myself in my studies.

The school was especially difficult in my first semester. I had to adjust to all of the assignments, school projects, and early morning classes. I was determined to succeed in getting my degree. After a month into the first semester, I adjusted and met a guy in one of my classes who was exactly my age. We got on well and became friends and study buddies.

One notable moment occurred during an

assignment given by our English professor, in which I chose to reflect briefly on my experiences during the civil war in my home country. Impressed by my resilience and positive demeanor, she encouraged me to share my story with a broader audience, suggesting that it could inspire and uplift others.

Grateful for her encouragement, I took her advice to heart. Six years later, I finally decided to write down my experiences in this book as a tribute to my journey and a beacon of hope for those facing adversity.

In 2019, I graduated with a bachelor's degree in management, marking the culmination of my university journey in Canada.

# CHAPTER 9:
## MAKING THE MOVE AND MANAGING EXPECTATIONS

This chapter is dedicated to young professionals contemplating a move from Africa to North America, specifically to Canada or the United States. Below are insights and cautionary advice for those considering such a transition, drawn from my personal experience.

To individuals in their forties with stable jobs in Africa, I strongly advise you to research before relocating. While the allure of a new life abroad may seem promising, the reality often differs from our expectations. Transitioning to life in the United States or Canada demands meticulous mental, physical, and emotional preparation. Patience, perseverance, and hard work are essential virtues, as the adjustment period can be protracted and challenging.

While Canada and the United States boast remarkable beauty and ample opportunities for growth and development, achieving success in these countries requires time and effort. It is crucial to dispel the notion that success will come swiftly and effortlessly upon arrival.

Reflecting on my own journey, I acknowledge the trials and tribulations faced both in Canada and the United States. These adversities ultimately contributed to my personal growth and development, but they are not to be considered lightly.

After graduating from the University of

Lethbridge, I have had the privilege of working for several reputable companies with increasing remuneration. At present, I hold a managerial position with the Government of Yukon. Despite the challenges encountered along the way, I am grateful to call this beautiful country my home, where I will continue to strive for personal and professional fulfillment and, in my little way, serve the community I live. Thank you for taking the time to read my story. I hope it inspires you. This book is a testament of courage, determination, hard work, and resilience.

# CHAPTER 10:
## SIX PRINCIPLES OF RESILIENCE

## Principle 1: Hope: A Light in the Darkness

In the heart of Sierra Leone's civil war, hope was not merely an abstract idea; it was necessary for survival. The war ravaged the land and tore apart families. Entire communities were forced into displacement and despair. In such moments, hope was a refuge for me and my family.

I anchored my hope in the belief that the war would one day end and peace would eventually return to my shattered homeland. My mom clung to hope as she shielded me and my siblings from the horrors around us, telling us stories of a brighter future to keep our young spirits alive. Amidst the constant threat of violence, hope was the fuel that inspired me to flee to safety, seek refuge, and take steps to rebuild despite relentless setbacks.

Even in the darkest moments, symbols of hope endured. Songs were sung softly in the night, prayers were shared in hushed voices, and acts of kindness reaffirmed our shared humanity. These fragments of hope wove into a tapestry of resilience, which enabled me and my family to hold on when everything else seemed lost.

Darkness is often where hope shines the brightest. During times of great uncertainty, when the future feels like an insurmountable void, hope provides the courage to take the next step forward.

Imagine me and my family fleeing through dense forests, hearing the distant echoes of gunfire, a chilling reminder of the peril we escaped. We had no guarantees of safety, no knowledge of what lay ahead, and yet we pressed on. The beacon guiding us through this treacherous terrain was hope; if we could survive another day, we might find peace, a home, or even reunite with loved ones.

For me, hope was not merely optimism; it was a rebellion against despair. It defied logic and circumstances and urged me to focus on the slivers of possibility rather than the overwhelming odds. Even in the presence of fear, it refused to yield. Hope fortified my spirit when tragedy threatened to extinguish it.

In *Resilience: From Civil War to The Canadian Dream*, hope is both the anchor that held me steady and the compass that pointed me toward a better tomorrow.

Whether amid war, personal loss, or the challenges of starting over, hope provides a reason to persevere. It reminds us that no matter how dark the night, dawn is always just over the horizon.

Hope is the foundation of resilience, an enduring source of strength in the face of adversity. It sustained me, my family, and the people of Sierra Leone through the devastation of war. It continues to inspire me as we pursue dreams of peace, stability, and fulfillment. Hope transformed my life shaped by conflict into one marked by purpose—a story that now stands as a testament to the power of hope to carry me forward, even in the most challenging of times.

## Principle 2   - Pivoting: Adapting in the Face of Life's Challenges

Life, like the unpredictable winds of a storm, often forces us to navigate uncharted waters. Survival frequently depends on the ability to pivot—changing course when the path ahead becomes impassable. This principle, rooted in resilience, was key in my journey when an unforeseen detour redirected my life from America to Canada.

My initial move to the United States from Sierra Leone felt like a triumph. After surviving the devastation of civil war, arriving in a land of opportunity seemed like the culmination of a dream. I had envisioned building a stable life there, but as time went on, I found myself navigating obstacles I hadn't anticipated. These obstacles chipped away at the foundation of the dream I had carefully constructed.

In my experience, pivoting is never easy, especially when it involves uprooting one's life. It requires leaving comfort zones, familiar surroundings, and aspirations tied to a specific place or goal. I wrestled with the idea of relocating to Canada. It felt like admitting defeat, as if I was abandoning the hope I had. Then I realized that resilience is not about stubbornly clinging to one path; it is about courageously seeking another when circumstances demand it.

Through this experience, I came to understand that pivoting is not just an act of survival, but an act of self-empowerment. It taught me to:

- **Recognize when change is necessary:** Ignoring the signs that a situation is untenable only prolongs suffering. The decision to pivot must be rooted in self-awareness and a willingness to face reality.

- **Embrace uncertainty:** Pivoting requires stepping into the unknown. While this can be terrifying, it is also an opportunity for growth and discovery.

- **Redefine success:** Success is not always about achieving a specific goal. Sometimes, it's about finding a new path that aligns better with your values and circumstances.

- **Cultivate resilience:** Each pivot strengthens my ability to adapt, reinforcing my capacity to handle future challenges.

Looking back, the move to Canada marked one of the most significant pivots of my life. It reshaped my understanding of resilience and taught me that true strength lies in flexibility. What began as a painful departure from a long-held dream evolved into a gateway to a new opportunity—not only for myself, but for my family.

As I reflect on my journey from Sierra Leone to the United States and ultimately to Canada, I am reminded that life is not a straight road, but a series of winding paths. Each detour, while challenging, has brought me closer to the person I was meant to become. Pivoting is not a sign of weakness; it is a testament to our ability to persevere.

If there is one lesson, I hope readers take from this principle, it is this: never be afraid to pivot. When the road ahead seems blocked, trust in your ability to chart a new course. Growth does not come from resisting change but from embracing it with open arms.

In the end, it is not the challenges that define a person but how one responds to them. Pivoting, as painful as it may be, is a declaration of hope, a reminder that, even in the face of adversity, we hold the power to reshape our destiny.

This principle serves as both a reflection on my own journey and a guide for anyone facing similar crossroads. Through the principle of pivoting, I was able to survive and thrive.

## Principle 3: Faith: Anchoring the Spirit Amid Uncertainty

Resilience is often portrayed as a combination of determination, strength, and the ability to persevere through hardship. But, at its core, resilience requires faith—a trust in something greater than oneself, a belief in the unseen, and the conviction that despite life's darkest moments, light lies ahead. For me, faith was not just one principle of resilience; it was the foundation upon which I built my survival and eventual triumph. Faith in God, faith in myself, faith in my family—these were the anchors that kept me grounded amid chaos and propelled me toward hope and healing.

## Faith in God

In the darkest days of the Sierra Leone Civil War, where every sound of gunfire threatened to be the last, I turned to God in prayer for courage, strength, and hope.

When the world around me fell into violence and despair, my faith in God gave me a reason to hold on. I believed that there was a higher purpose for my life, even when my surroundings screamed otherwise. This belief was not born out of naïve optimism, but out of necessity. Faith was my shield against the despair that could have swallowed me whole.

Years later, as I found myself navigating a new life in Canada, far from the soil of my birth, that same faith in God reminded me that I was not alone. I found a church community that welcomed me, and through prayer and fellowship, I rediscovered the strength that had carried me through my childhood. Faith in God was my constant, an anchor in both war and peace, reminding me to trust in my relationship with Him, even when I couldn't see the full picture.

## Faith in Myself

It is one thing to have faith in God, but it is

equally important to have faith in oneself. For years, I doubted my worth. The trauma of war left scars, and moving to Canada presented its own challenges—cultural differences, financial struggles, and the constant pressure to provide for my mother and siblings back home.

Somewhere along the journey, I learned that resilience begins with believing in your own ability to rise above adversity. It wasn't easy. I had to remind myself every day that I was capable of building a new life. Each small victory—finding a job, learning new skills, building relationships—strengthened my confidence.

Faith in myself didn't mean ignoring my flaws or pretending I had all the answers. It meant accepting that I was a work in progress, capable of growth and adaptation. It was the belief that I was not defined by my past but by the choices I made moving forward.

## Faith in My Mom

If faith is learned, then my first teacher was my mother. Her unwavering strength during the war, her relentless prayers, and her belief that her children could rise above their circumstances shaped me profoundly. She taught me that faith is not just about waiting for miracles; it's acting in alignment with that belief.

I remember her shielding us from chaos, even when her own heart must have been breaking. She had an incredible ability to remain hopeful, to believe in a future that seemed impossible in those moments. Her faith became my faith. She was my example of resilience, and her strength was a reminder that love and faith could transcend the horrors of war.

As I navigated life in Canada, my mother's voice remained with me. I could hear her encouraging me to push forward, to trust in God and myself, and to believe in the power of family. Even now, her faith shines like a beacon, reminding me of the sacrifices she made and the lessons she imparted.

## Faith in My Siblings

Surviving as a family during the war required not only individual strength, but collective faith. My siblings and I became each other's support system, leaning on one another in ways that deepened our bond.

There were times when survival seemed impossible, but together, we chose to believe in a better future. We shared stories, dreams, and moments of laughter amid the chaos. That shared faith—that unspoken agreement that we would endure—was a powerful force.

## The Power of Faith in Resilience

Faith is not a passive concept; it is active, dynamic, and deeply personal. For me, it was trusting in God's character, believing in my own ability to overcome, and relying on the love of my family. It was a reminder that even in the midst of uncertainty, God could bring purpose out of pain and provide a path to healing.

Faith anchored my spirit during the Civil War and propelled me toward the Canadian dream. It reminded me that resilience is not just about enduring hardship, but about believing in something greater—whether that's a higher power, one's own potential, or the people who stand by one's side.

Faith has been my constant companion, connecting moments of despair with moments of triumph, like an unseen thread. Faith has taught me to trust, to hope, and to persevere.

## Principle 4: Adaptability: Thriving Through Change

The transition from living in a home to surviving in a refugee camp was abrupt and unsettling. Refugee camps are generally characterized by scarcity, overcrowding, and an overwhelming sense of loss. Yet, for me, it also became the place where adaptability was forged and tested.

Adapting to camp life also meant navigating new forms of community. In displacement, boundaries between people are blurred. Strangers became family, and diverse languages and cultures intertwined. I learned to negotiate these differences, using gestures and the universal language of kindness to build bonds.

The move to the United States brought a new layer of complexity. It was a place of abundance compared to the scarcity I had endured, but it was also a place of stark cultural differences. The hustle of life, its obsession with individualism, and its technological advancements were overwhelming and exhilarating.

In those early days, adaptability meant observing, learning, and mimicking. I remember struggling with simple things, such as how to navigate a grocery store with endless aisles of unfamiliar products and understanding the unwritten rules of social interaction. Adapting to the culture didn't mean abandoning my identity; it meant finding a balance between who I was and who I needed to become in order to succeed in this new country.

The United States also taught me the value of opportunity. In this place, adaptability meant seizing every chance to learn, grow, and contribute. It wasn't easy — there were moments of doubt and homesickness — but each challenge became a stepping stone and taught me resilience in a new context.

Moving to Canada in 2012 was the beginning of a new chapter for me. It was a place to settle, build, and dream, but this transition required adaptability as well. Canada's cold winters, diverse cultures, and emphasis on multiculturalism were an entirely new experience.

The first winter was a trial by fire, or rather by ice. Coming from a warm climate, I wasn't prepared for the bone-chilling cold. Adapting required me to learn how to dress in layers, shovel snow, and navigate icy sidewalks. Beyond the physical climate, adapting to Canada meant understanding its social fabric.

In Canada, adaptability was about integration without assimilation. It meant contributing to a society that valued diversity while staying true to my roots. I joined community groups, volunteered at local organizations, and shared my story to inspire others. I embraced the Canadian values of politeness, inclusivity, and strong work ethic, but I also contributed to the values of Sierra Leonean hospitality, resilience, and community spirit.

Building a career in Canada required a different type of adaptability. My experiences as a refugee didn't align well with Canadian job expectations, so I had to upskill, retrain, and start from scratch in many ways. Yet, this process taught me that adaptability is not about lowering one's standards, but about finding new ways to achieve one's goals.

## Personal Lessons in Adaptability

- **Embrace Uncertainty:** Refugee camps and migrations taught me to face the unknown with courage.
- **Find Balance:** Staying rooted in my Sierra Leonean identity while embracing new cultures allowed me to build a unique perspective.
- **Seize Opportunities:** Adaptability means being ready to act when opportunities arise, even if they take you out of your comfort zone.

Adaptability is another thread that weaves through my journey. It is what enabled me to survive the civil war, endure displacement, and build a new life in Canada. It is a principle that I pass on to my children, my community, and now to you, the reader. Life will always throw challenges our way, but with adaptability, we can not only overcome them, but transform them into opportunities for growth and transformation.

## Principle 5: Patience: Enduring the Process with Grace

Patience is often perceived as a quiet virtue, one that requires holding back in the face of adversity or waiting for the right moment to act. Yet, for me, patience is not a passive act; it is a force of resilience. Patience is enduring the process of life with grace. Though the road may be long, the rewards that come at the end are worth every moment of waiting.

During times of conflict, such as the civil war in Sierra Leone, patience is a matter of survival. Each day is marked by uncertainty, and the future seems like a distant, unreachable dream. In such circumstances, patience is an internal force that helps one withstand the unbearable. It is not about surrendering to passivity but rather about holding onto hope, no matter how slight it might be, and waiting for a time when peace will return.

Amid the chaos of war, patience was an act of resistance. It is through patience that I refused to be broken by circumstances beyond my control. It is through patience that I preserved my dignity, my dreams, and my belief in a future free from violence. I waited for peace, not in idleness, but with purpose, and took each step toward a new beginning, no matter how small.

When forced to flee my home due to war, I often faced uncertainty in refugee and displaced persons camps. I waited for an opportunity to rebuild my life. For me, this waiting period was agonizing, yet essential to the process of resilience. The journey of a refugee is long, and the promise of a new life in a new land often feels distant. It is in these moments of waiting that patience becomes a powerful tool for mental and emotional endurance.

The principle of patience teaches that the time spent waiting is never wasted. For every challenge faced during the adjustment period, there is an opportunity for growth.

One of the greatest challenges in the practice of patience is learning to embrace the small victories along the way. Often, the rewards for enduring hardship and waiting for change are not immediately apparent. It can be tempting to become disheartened when progress seems slow or when setbacks arise. Patience taught me that it is the accumulation of small wins that eventually leads to greater success.

In my journey from surviving the war to realizing the Canadian dream, each small success—whether mastering a new skill, finding a job, or making a new friend—became a milestone that proved resilience was taking root. Every moment of patience was a step toward building the life that was once only a dream. Through these small, everyday victories, I developed the skills I needed to succeed and the confidence to keep moving forward.

The resilience built through patience is what allows me to appreciate the journey, not just the destination.

Patience does not mean waiting passively; it

means engaging with the process of change and finding ways to grow during the waiting period. It is through patience that the journey becomes just as important as the destination. It is through patience that I learned not only to survive, but to thrive.

The story of resilience is not simply about overcoming challenges; it is about enduring them with grace. Patience allows me to maintain that grace, even when the future is uncertain. In the end, the rewards of patience — peace, security, and a new life in a foreign land — are worth every moment of the wait.

## Principle 6: Positivity: A Mindset Focused on Possibilities

In the darkest hours, a positive mindset transforms setbacks into stepping stones, paving the way toward hope and renewal. The principle of positivity is a cornerstone of resilience. A constructive attitude in the midst of adversity can lead to unimaginable breakthroughs.

Positivity is more than wishful thinking or blind optimism; it is an intentional shift in perspective where obstacles are reframed as opportunities. This mindset does not ignore pain or hardship; rather, it chooses to see a path forward despite them. At its core, positivity acknowledges reality but refuses to be confined by it. It is the belief that every trial holds a lesson, and every setback is a setup for a comeback.

The civil war in Sierra Leone was a storm that uprooted lives, shattered communities, and tested the resolve of millions. I was surrounded by destruction, fear, and despair. Friends and family were lost, and the future seemed bleak. It would have been easy to succumb to hopelessness. Yet, even in those moments, I found sparks of light.

I remember one particular day during the war when food was scarce, and the sound of gunfire was ever-present. My mother, an unyielding source of strength, said to me, "Today, we will smile. Not because life is easy, but because we are alive to see another day." Her words became my mantra. Instead of dwelling on the things we lacked, we focused on small victories—finding shelter and helping a neighbor in need. These simple acts of hope reminded us that even in chaos, life still held meaning.

Through this lens of positivity, I saw the resilience in my community. People who had lost everything began rebuilding, not because they had to, but because they believed in the possibility of a better tomorrow.

I use the following exercises to stay positive in difficult situations:

> **Practice Gratitude**: In difficult times, it's easy to focus on what's wrong. I take a moment each day to reflect on something positive, no matter how small. Gratitude shifts my focus from scarcity to abundance and helps me see the good that still exists.

> **Reframe Challenges**: When faced with setbacks, I ask myself, "What can I learn from this?" Viewing the problem as an opportunity for growth reduces stress and fosters resilience.

> **Surround Yourself with Optimism:** The people you surround yourself with significantly impact your mindset. I

seek out those who uplift and encourage me.

> **Visualize**: Picture the outcome you desire. I focus on a positive vision for the future that motivates me to work toward it, even when the present feels overwhelming.

> **Practice Kindness**: Helping others can be a powerful way to reinforce positivity. It shifts my focus from my personal struggles to the collective good and reminds me of my ability to make a difference.

As I reflect on my journey from surviving a civil war to building a life in Canada, I realize that positivity was not only a mindset; it was a lifeline. It helped me to see beyond my circumstances, to believe in the possibility of change, and to act on that belief.

Positivity allowed me to look at the rubble of my life and see the foundation for something new. It transformed my pain into progress, despair into determination, and challenges into catalysts for change.

As you navigate your own trials, remember that a positive attitude will not eliminate diffi-culty, but it will illuminate the path forward. Like a steady light in a dark tunnel, positivity will guide you to the other side, where possibilities await.

Keep this principle close to your heart as you walk your own journey of resilience. When the world says, "You can't," let your positivity respond, "Watch me."

# PHOTO OF MY MOM

*Me and my mother at Koidu City, Kono District,*

*Sierra Leone*

# PHOTO OF MY DAD

My late dad, Chief Kembay. This picture was taken in the early 70s and is the remaining image I have of him.

www.ingramcontent.com/pod-product-compliance
Lightning Source LLC
Chambersburg PA
CBHW051503050726
47593CB00005B/2203